EXIST N

The Art Of Squeezing The Most Out Of Life

Detavio Samuels

Dedicated to Tanya (the love of my life), Mom, Dad, Mike, Kim, Tanner, and Bryanna. I love you all dearly.

TABLE OF CONTENTS

MAKE IT HAPPEN | 67

PARTING WORDS | 99

INTRODUCTION

READ IT

Freedom is useless if we do not exercise it as characters making choices… We are free to change the stories by which we live. Because we are genuine characters, and not mere puppets, we can choose our defining stories. We can do so because we actively participate in the creation of our stories. We are co-authors as well as characters. Few things are as encouraging as the realization that things can be different and that we have a role in making them so.
—DANIEL TAYLOR

We define ourselves by the choices we have made. We are, in fact, the sum-total of our choices.
—WOODY ALLEN

As a child, I once asked a group of adults why God chose to make man after He had already created angels. I didn't understand why God would want to make human beings when He already had such magnificent and beautiful creatures that endlessly praised, served, and glorified Him. Why would God waste His time gambling on men when He already had an army of angelic beings He could count on? I received the following answer: God wanted to create beings that had free will, and that would have to choose to serve Him.

I tell you this story because it points to one of the defining characteristics of mankind: we are blessed with the power of choice. We can do or not do. We can accept the path we are on or alter our individual journeys. Every second of every day, each and every one of us has the power to write his or her own story, create our own path, and step into the future we desire—all because we have the ability to choose. Different choices will determine different paths.

Exist No More is about choices. It is filled with short and simple ideas to push you, incite you, and arm you so that you can make choices that will lead you to your brightest future. It will encourage you not to accept what life has seemingly handed you as final, but to dare to be bold enough to make the important decisions that will create your happiest and most impactful life. It will inspire you to choose not to let your gifts go to waste but to unleash your personal magic on the world. It will equip you with tools to make choices that will help you unglue yourself on the days where you find yourself stuck.

Exist No More was written to provoke you to choose a path that leads away from a dull and mediocre existence and toward one that helps you pursue an inspired and passion-filled life. This book is meant to be a helpful guide along your personal journey to self-fulfillment and growth.

I chose to write *Exist No More* for you; I hope you choose to read it.

UNLEASH YOUR MAGIC

Everything you need to live an extraordinary and impactful life is already inside of you. But in order to set the world on fire, you must first acknowledge your gifts, believe in yourself, and set your aims high.

Get Turned On!

If you don't wake up in the morning excited to pick up where you left your work yesterday, you haven't found your calling yet.
—*Mike Wallace*

Don't ask yourself what the world needs. Ask yourself what makes you come alive, and go do that, because what the world needs is people who have come alive.
—*Howard Thurman*

You are designed to be ON.

By ON I mean awake. Inspired. Made alive by doing the work you love.

By ON I mean your work is so well-aligned with your natural gifts and passions you find it difficult to understand where the pleasure stops and work begins. Where the very thing that consumes you is the same thing that feeds you energy. Where you are so engaged in what you do, you find it difficult to "turn off."

You are supposed to be ON.

By ON I mean doing your very best work always. Operating at a level where you are dangerously good and exceptionally creative.

Unfortunately, most people never experience what it is like to be ON. As a whole, most of us have settled for OFF in exchange for social acceptance, validation of the degrees we've worked hard to earn, or the comfort of not having to do the hard work necessary to figure out what excites us. Sadly, as a society, we've accepted OFF as the norm and made ON the exception. The end result is a culture of mediocrity. Refuse to fit in.

You are wired to be ON.

When you are ON, you make those around you better. By your genius. By your creativity. By your strength.

No one needs another mismatched employee—another square peg in a round hole. We need you to be ON.

MAKE ART

Art isn't pretty. Art isn't painting. Art isn't something you hang on the wall. Art is what we do when we're truly alive.
—*SETH GODIN*

Art enables us to find ourselves and lose ourselves at the same time.
—*THOMAS MERTON*

We all start out as artists. As children, we have an unrestrained imagination and a desire to create. We develop kingdoms with Legos, we imagine fortresses with blankets, and we draw never-before-seen worlds with paint, pens, and pencils. As children, we are proud to call ourselves artists.

But somewhere along the way, things change and we lose our claim on the creative world of our youth. We forfeit our natural gifts as artists, not because we have suddenly lost our talent to create, but because we adopt a definition of who and what an artist is that does not include us.

As a result of our formal education, we come to associate the term "artist" with what we are told are the fine arts. Its practitioners include visual artists, sculptors, painters, musicians, dancers, and others we associate with the exceptionally talented members of the creative class. We reserve and associate art with people that wear berets, drink fine wines, and possess some magical creative ability that we assume can only be inspired by the gods.

But we're wrong. Although we stop recognizing ourselves as artists, we never actually lose our ability to make art.

Deep down, we are all still artists.

When we enter the world of creativity and inspiration, we become engaged in creating art. Art is what we do when we create things that previously did not exist. Art is what we do when we are being our best selves, whether that's developing a business strategy, making a home-cooked meal or creating a classroom-atmosphere where young, moldable minds come alive. Whatever brings you to life while bringing out the best in you *is* your art!

Although it took me a long time to see myself as an artist, I can now find art in almost everything I do. As an advertising executive, art is in the stories I build for my clients. As a writer, art is in the words that fill this page. As one who lives their life in the public eye, art is in my social media updates that broadcast my life's journey with the hope that I will be a living example that anything is possible.

I am an artist.

And so are you.

Find your artistic voice. Practice and perfect your craft. And then leave your art in places where it will challenge conventions or continue to change the world long after you are gone.

DREAM BIG

*All men dream: but not equally. Those who dream by night in the
dusty recesses of their minds wake in the day to find that it was
vanity: but the dreamers of the day are dangerous men, for
they may act their dream with open eyes, to make it possible.*
—*T. E. LAWRENCE*

*A person often becomes what he believes himself to be. If I keep on
saying to myself that I cannot do a certain thing, it is possible that
I may end by really becoming incapable of doing it. On the
contrary, if I have the belief that I can do it, I shall surely acquire
the capacity to do it, even if I may not have it at the beginning.*
—*MOHANDAS GANDHI*

Dreams set the bar for what we hope and expect out of life; they
ultimately become incredibly accurate predictors of who we will
eventually become. Dream big and you will achieve big things.
Dream small and expect small results. It is not that big dreamers
are more capable than other people, it's just that no one can hope
to accomplish more than he or she can imagine.

Dreaming big can be unnerving. Dreams have a unique way of
making us feel vulnerable, exposed, and open to disappointment.
The higher our hopes and aspirations, the farther we can fall.

And so we have to become brave people, willing to open our hearts and minds to the possibility of what *could be*, even if it means risking failure along the way.

Big dreamers get the big payoffs not because they are better at doing something, but because they are courageous. It takes courage to dream the kind of dreams that set your soul on fire—the kind of aspirations or ideas that keep you up at night. It takes courage to dream the type of dreams that make you intolerant of where you are today, and make you impatient to see yourself anywhere else than in the life you have imagined.

Your dreams and aspirations are not meant to be static. They are dynamic and meant to evolve. As you grow, your dreams must grow with you and reflect the totality of your life experience. The dreams you had at the age of five should not be the only dreams you still have today.

The key to helping your dreams progress is exposing yourself to things that stretch beyond what you currently know to be possible. Inject yourself into new cultures. Explore different ideas and opportunities. Make friendships across ethnic, religious, and economic lines. You cannot dream of what you do not know, but the more you know the more you dream.

Dream big for your family. Dream big for your business. Dream big for yourself. If you are going to do something amazing, it's going to start with the size of your dreams.

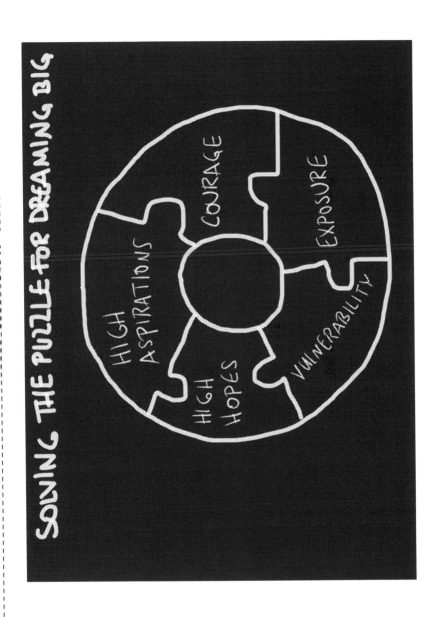

Discover Yourself

Maturity includes the recognition that no one is going to see anything in us that we don't see in ourselves. Stop waiting for a producer. Produce yourself.
—Marianne Williamson

Change will not come if we wait for some other person or if we wait for some other time. We are the ones we've been waiting for.
—Barack Obama

Our world is marked by rapid change. A decade ago if you had a big idea, you were forced to deal with middlemen to make it a reality. Middlemen were often investors, big retailers, or major publishers that made millions by forcing dreamers to go through them to see a dream become a reality. If you needed money, you had to pitch and land venture capital. If you wanted your product to sell, you had to convince big retailers that it would make them tons of money before they would put your product on the shelf. If you wanted to get your thoughts out, you had to go through a publishing house to be able to get your words into print.

These middlemen had all of the power and therefore were in control of capital, commerce, and culture. Any idea that did not go through them simply would not materialize. And to get past them, you first had to be "discovered."

Being discovered was not easy. There were no rules. There was no formula to follow. Being discovered only happened with a wish, a prayer, and luck.

Today, things are different. Thanks largely to technology, the game is changing and the barriers to being discovered are eroding. The $10,000 piece of musical equipment it took to create that magical "studio sound" on an album can now be mimicked with a $10 computer program. The millions of people that marketers drew with their brick-and-mortar stores can now be reached online with a shoestring budget, thanks to social media and online retailers like Etsy, Amazon, and Shopify. And the thousands of dollars you once needed to raise from venture capitalists and wealthy investors can now be generated from complete strangers without any exchange of equity through platforms like Kickstarter and Indiegogo.

Today the middleman is losing his control, and power is shifting into the hands of extraordinary people like you and me. You no longer have to wait for access to the right stage, people, or tools. The only thing you have to wait on is for you to discover yourself.

Uncover Your Magic

He who knows others is wise; he who knows himself is enlightened.
—*Lao Tzu*

All it takes is all you got.
—*Marc Davis*

If you want to understand the purpose of something, you first need to look at its designer's intent. Whether you are talking about the wheels on a car or the pollen-carrying body of a bumblebee, the creator's purpose is always revealed in the makeup of his or her creation. This is true for humans as well.

If you want to understand why you are here on earth, you must first examine who you are on the inside. There are no accidents. There are no mistakes. Everything you need to be great is already inside of you. The passions that keep you awake at night, the ideas that won't allow you to sleep, even the personality quirks you brought along with you the moment you entered the world—all of these things are a purposeful part of YOUR design and combine to form your own personal magic.

Identifying your magic is difficult—not because it is an impossible task but because we navigate through life with an external orientation. Instead of looking inside to uncover our own magic we spend much of our time idolizing the magic we so easily see in others. Attracted to those who have superpowers we may not possess, our external disposition not only distracts us from seeing our own greatness but also creates perceptions of personal deficiency and lack.

Do not spend too much time studying others; it will only lead you to obsess with your perceived disqualifications. You are uniquely qualified to do exactly what you have been put here to do.

Do not become bewitched by the magic of others; uncover your own magic.

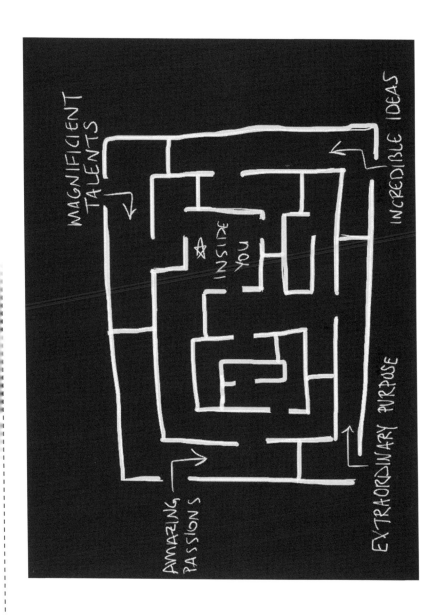

BE READY TO QUIT

The only way to define your limits is by going beyond them.
—ANONYMOUS

Any life worth living begins with confusion and returns to that confusion again and again. The trick is to feel at home in that uncertainty and allow a new pattern—a new approach—to unfold.
—DAN WIEDEN

There should be times when you are ready to quit. There should be nights when you are ready to pull your hair out. There should be moments when your inner voice tells you that you cannot go on. There should definitely be times when you have had enough. Whether it's a new project, your training regimen, or the effort you put into your relationship with your spouse—there should be times when you feel you just cannot take the monumental challenges you face anymore.

That is when and how you know you are pushing yourself. That is when and how you know you are testing yourself. That is when and how you know you are on the brink of growth, achievement, and discovery. In fact, the only way you will uncover your true capabilities is to live at the limit of what you believe to be your potential.

The only way to know you are on the verge of greatness is if the challenges you face constantly cause you to have to convince yourself not to walk away.

During your youth these moments were manufactured for you. They came in a variety of forms: your algebra homework, competitive sports, ballet lessons, and a host of other challenges the adults in your life forced you to do. But now you are an adult and no one—besides yourself—is responsible for pushing your boundaries so that you can see, really *see*, who you are.

If you are not ready to quit, you are probably sitting too comfortably in the welcoming arms of complacence, habit, and ordinariness. If you are not ready to quit, you are probably not measuring up to all that you truly can be.

If you are testing the boundaries of what you know to be possible, then at some point, you will be ready to quit.

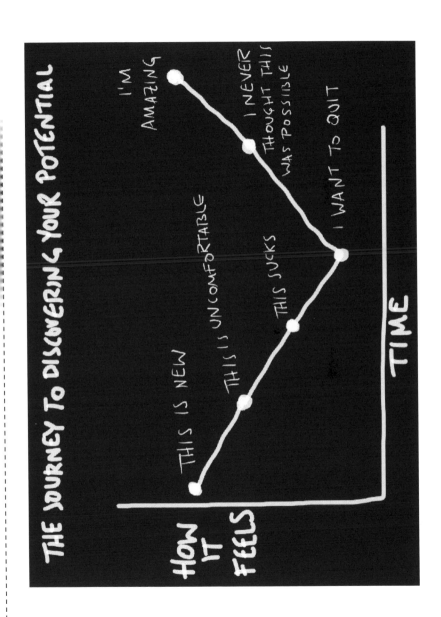

.

THINK DIFFERENTLY

Living life to the fullest will sometimes mean following different rules than everybody else.

REJECT AUTOPILOT

We don't think about what we're doing. We drift along in life, floating on the wake of past choices, and it's easy to forget that we have the ability to change direction.
— CHIP AND DAN HEATH, DECISIVE

An idea is like a virus—resilient, highly contagious. The smallest seed of an idea can grow. It can grow to define or destroy you.
—DOM COBB, INCEPTION

Ideas are the most powerful things in this world. They move everything. Ideas can save lives, capture the hearts and minds of a nation, and create billion-dollar enterprises. Nothing is stronger than the power of an idea.

Ideas do not only move things, they also move people.

I love the movie *Inception* because it brings this truth to life. In the movie, the main character, Dom Cobb, played by Leonardo DiCaprio, is hired to plant an idea inside the mind of a businessman. Cobb and his team pull off the job by diving several layers down into their target's dreams so they can plant the new idea deep enough for it to actually take root and start dictating his decision-making when he wakes up.

Real life mirrors this fictional process. How you see yourself, everything you believe, what roles you desire to play in life—all are the results of ideas that were planted in your mind by the people around you. Some were planted carefully and purposefully, others not so much.

Most seeds are planted while you are awake. Someone tells you that you are not good enough, you are too fat, you cannot make money doing what you love. Whatever the idea, it has taken root and now makes up the fabric of who you are. It causes you to make daily decisions with little thought behind what you are doing or why you are doing it.

Start questioning the ideas that drive your behaviors. You may find out some of the ideas that move you are still valid. But you may determine some ideas are antiquated, inaccurate, or no longer valuable at this stage in your life.

One way to do this is to sit down with a pen and paper and pick an idea that tends to recur in your mind. For example: You want to be a doctor, you cannot depend on anyone, if you were a "good wife" you would cook and clean more. Whatever the idea, write it down.

Next, employ a technique called laddering. Essentially, laddering is to pretend you are having a conversation with one of those annoying five-year-olds who cannot stop asking "Why?" Regardless of how great an answer you give, he or she will always follow it up with another "Why?" In this exercise, you are simultaneously the adult and the five-year-old. Pick an idea and start asking yourself why it is important to you until you reach some sort of an "Aha!" moment.

The next step is to question that idea's validity. If after vetting the idea it still makes sense to you, keep it. But if it does not, get rid of it. Uproot the old plant so that you can make room for a new one to grow.

Do not be afraid to start questioning things. It is never too late to get off autopilot and begin understanding what ideas control your behavior. Only you can determine if the ideas you have adopted are driving you toward greatness or destruction. Introspection helps you decide whether an idea should be allowed to flourish, or if it is time for it to be weeded out.

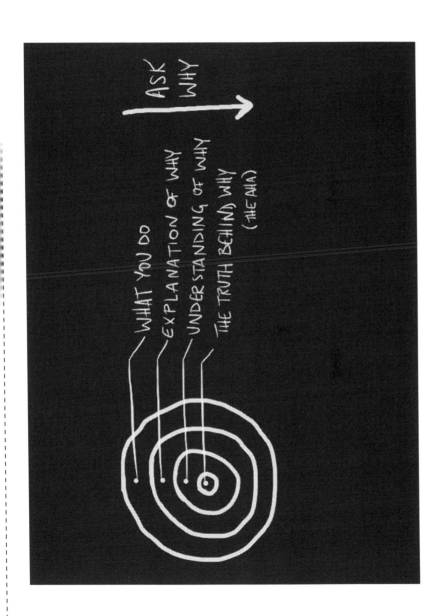

Do Not Give
Everything Your All

Quality is never an accident.
It is always the result of intelligent effort.
—*John Ruskin*

For every disciplined effort there is a multiple reward.
—*Jim Rohn*

When I worked at Johnson & Johnson, my boss told me I had one major problem: I always gave 110 percent to every assignment. I remember being baffled as the words came out of his mouth. What employer does not want his employee to give 110 percent every time?

In my past, giving my all each and every time I "stepped on the court" was a part of who I was. This was what made me special. This was what made me valuable. Now, all of a sudden, I was on a team that didn't value my 110 percent philosophy. I drew the conclusion that perhaps I was playing on the wrong team.

I was told to gauge the amount of effort required for a given assignment and only deliver what was necessary. There were times when my boss wanted me to trade my best work for speed: give him

C+ work and complete a task in fifteen minutes versus taking a whole day to deliver A+ work. There were assignments in which he wanted me to do the minimum amount necessary so that it would not interfere with a more critical assignment I was working on simultaneously: give him C+ work on a low-profile assignment so that I could have more to time to deliver A+ work on a high-profile assignment.

And that's when I learned that nothing requires your best, 100 percent of the time!

Time is a fixed asset. Once you use it, you lose it. Identify the meaningless things that you can accomplish without an amazing amount of effort so you can have more time and give your best energy to the things that matter. For example, your wife. Or your prayer life. Or the idea you've been itching to launch.

Life is cluttered with a bunch time-sucking tasks and distractions. Do not let the insignificant things steal time from the things that actually matter. Just because you are used to giving your all does not mean you have to every time.

EFFORT FRAMEWORK

HIGH IMPACT

LOW IMPACT

HIGH URGENCY

LOW URGENCY

TAKE YOUR TIME; DO YOUR BEST

THE BEST YOU CAN IN THE TIME YOU'VE GOT

QUESTION WHETHER THIS NEEDS TO BE DONE AT ALL

JUST ENOUGH TO GET THIS OFF YOUR PLATE (W/O DAMAGING REPUTATION)

Screw Weaknesses

Once we know our weaknesses they cease to do us any harm.
—Georg C. Lichtenberg

Damage control can prevent failure,
but it will never elevate you to excellence.
—Donald O. Clifton

Our educational system and society as a whole train us to spend an inordinate amount of time and energy trying to rid ourselves of our so-called "problem areas." Although teachers and mentors sometimes talk about classes in which students get As, they spend the bulk of their focus on classes where students get Cs and Ds. During a formal review process, bosses also overemphasize areas where improvement is needed instead of celebrating the places where employees exceed expectations. Over time, we are left with one clear message: The secret to getting ahead in life is to eliminate our weaknesses.

Rubbish. You cannot eliminate weaknesses. Research has shown that by your mid-teens your synaptic patterns—the formations of neurons in your brain that lead to your strengths—are formed and, for the most part, your strengths and weaknesses are anchored in stone. This means that if you are a terrible public speaker today, you will more than likely never be the next Barack Obama or Steve Jobs. It is not that you cannot work to overcome a weakness, but you will not be able to turn a real weakness into a true area of strength.

Spending too much time on your areas of weakness is a poor investment strategy; excelling in life is all that matters.

People hire for greatness. When is the last time you saw a job description from an employer who was looking for someone who was just "okay" at something? Chances are, you haven't. Job descriptions like that do not exist because people are not looking for "so-so," they are searching for mastery. People want to hire you because of what you are the best in the world at doing, not the worst. Consequently, if you have one additional hour to invest in yourself, nine out of ten times that hour will be best used by focusing on an area where you already excel—or have the potential for excellence. You separate yourself from the pack by moving from being good to great, not from bad to okay.

Fixing weaknesses is not a strategy for winning; it is a strategy for avoiding outright failure. You should focus on your problem areas only when your weaknesses are preventing you from delivering extraordinary outcomes. Otherwise, screw 'em! If a weakness does not stand in the way of your potential for greatness, then that weakness does not deserve your attention.

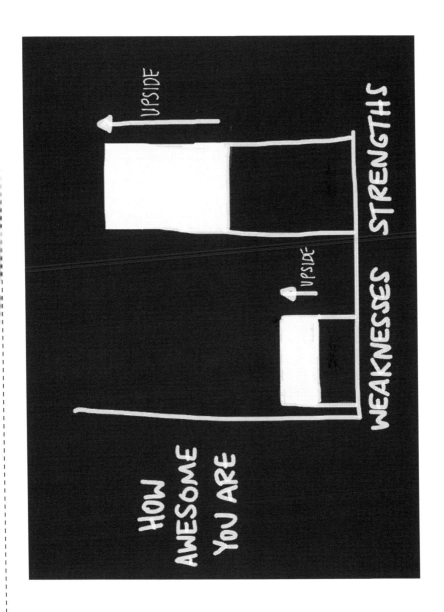

LIVE IN YOUR SWEET SPOT

*The most responsible, the most challenging, and, in the sense of
being true to yourself, the most honorable thing to do is face up to
the strength potential inherent in your talents and then
find ways to realize it.*
—DONALD O. CLIFTON

*Climbing to the top demands strength, whether it is to the top of
Mount Everest or to the top of your career.*
—ABDUL KALAM

I learned a lot during my time at the Stanford Graduate School
of Business, but one lesson stuck with me more than any other.
Two weeks before graduation, I had a "sit down" with three teachers who I believed were all living pieces of the dream I wanted
to create for myself. In an effort to avoid having theoretical conversations that would make me feel inspired in the moment, but
that I would quickly forget the second I walked out the room, I
prepared only one question for my teachers. I asked each profes-
sor to tell me the single most important thing he or she believed
was critical for me to do in order to propel myself forward in my
career.

I was surprised to discover that all three answers were a variation on the same theme: As quickly as possible and as often as you can, stop doing what you hate and only do what you love. In other words, each one recommended that I spend as much time as possible working in my "sweet spot."

In sports, the sweet spot is where a perfect combination of variables unite to enable the best possible outcome. In basketball, it is when a location on the court and a player's specific shooting style come together to make it all but impossible for that player to miss scoring. In baseball, it is the place where the batter's grip and the perfect placement of the bat against the ball come together to guarantee a home run. In your career, your sweet spot is the point where your unique attributes come together with the work you do on a daily basis to generate your highest possible level of performance.

Unique talents are the things that make you special; they are the gifts God has put inside you. You bring your unique elements to the table every time, without much thought or effort. These are the things that make you stand out from the crowd and, when put to work on the job, they simply make you better than your competition.

After completing business school, I went to work for Johnson & Johnson as an analyst. I was a fairly good analyst, but I knew I was definitely not in my sweet spot. Thankfully, God had the grace to remind me of this fact every day by partnering me with a colleague who was a better analyst than I would ever be. My partner ate, slept, and drank numbers, formulas, and spreadsheets. He loved what he did. He was in his sweet spot. Sure, I could have been promoted and achieved some level of success in that position, but I would never have become my best version of myself.

So I walked away from a future at Johnson & Johnson and looked for jobs that would allow me to put my gifts to full-time use. I ended up in advertising, where I have been promoted three times in five years and am one of the industry's youngest executives. I have been fortunate to accomplish in a short period what many in the industry never accomplish in a career. People always ask me how I was able to achieve such a so-called "meteoric rise to the top." To me, the answer is simple: I'm in a position where I am hard to beat. Not because I'm brilliant, but because I'm in my sweet spot.

Your curiosity level is high when you are in your sweet spot. Time disappears when you are in your sweet spot. You kick everyone else's butt when you are in your sweet spot.

In case you are struggling with finding and identifying what makes you special, here are a few places to start. Google *StrengthsFinder 2.0*, buy the book, and take the test inside. Then, talk to co-workers and the people closest to you about your results and see what they have to say about your greatest gifts and talents. Keep a personal journal to document the days you feel most alive and are happily consumed by what you are doing. Every few months, review your journal and search for patterns in the work you love.

Once you have identified your unique talents and passions, find a job that will allow you to spend at least 80 percent of your time doing what you love and are gifted at doing. Repeat this process over and over again every time you look for a new job. Enjoy the ride to the top. This is the path to happiness and excellence.

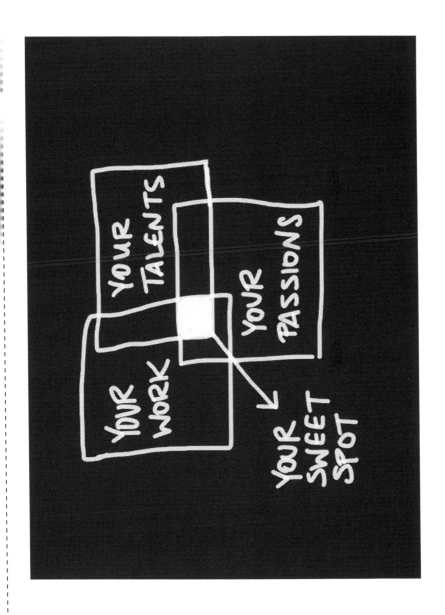

Explore Desire Paths

*Do not go where the path may lead, go instead where there is no
path and leave a trail.*
—RALPH WALDO EMERSON

*Two roads diverged in a wood, and I—
I took the one less traveled by, And that has made all the
difference.*
—ROBERT FROST, "THE ROAD NOT TAKEN"

Go to any park or forest and you will see at least two kinds of paths. The most noticeable paths are the "planner's paths"—the sidewalk or trail carefully designed by the park's creators. But if you keep looking, you'll also find "desire paths"—unofficial paths created in the same park by the footsteps of many who chose to create and travel on a different trajectory.

"Desire paths" are created for multiple reasons. Sometimes people recognize a shortcut to their destination. Other times they envision a new destination or find a new view, one that was not originally identified by the planners. Desirable destinations inevitably attract people to them. A desire path is born because someone recognizes a need for a new route—one that better suits his or her needs.

In life, we are generally taught to follow the "planner's path." It is a formulaic path that says: graduate from high school, go to college, get a graduate degree—because a college degree is no longer good enough—and a nice job. It is the path we are made to believe is the most reliable and safest. This course works well for most people; but, if there is anything the economy has taught us over the last few years, it is that no path is foolproof. No path leads to guaranteed success or comfort.

Explore the desire paths. Desire paths are all around you. They are the shortcuts created by curiosity, vision, and conviction. They are tracks laid down by those who decided the bigger risk is not in being unemployed, but in leaving their future in someone else's hands. These are the trails conceived in basements and garages where entrepreneurs tinker with new ideas, without fancy suits or degrees.

Don't blindly follow the planner's path. Observe the desire paths that have been created around you. These less-traveled, unofficial paths others have started just may suit you better. Do not be afraid to experiment with these trails—a little dirt can always be brushed off your sneakers.

The truly curious will also recognize that there are "desire paths" that have yet to be created. Do not be afraid to jump off the sidewalk or the footpath and be the first to pave a new way to success, either. Like Facebook's Mark Zuckerberg, Google's Sergey Brin or hip hop's Jay-Z, your tracks just may chart a course thousands of others are waiting follow.

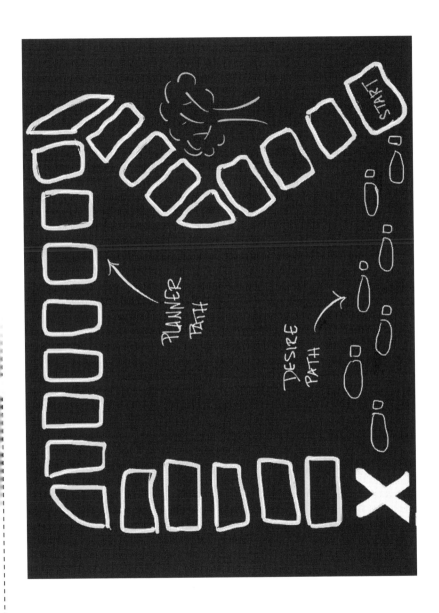

EDUCATE YOURSELF

Formal education makes you a living,
self-education makes you a legend.
—HABEEB AKANDE

Self-education is, I firmly believe,
the only kind of education there is.
—ISAAC ASIMOV

Teachers are amazing. As young students, we do not value them enough because we are too busy either hating school or trying to get all As. But to have someone who is dedicated, night and day, to ensuring that we learn everything we need know to make it to the next level and ultimately be successful in life is a rare and valuable gift. And on the day of our last class as seniors, we are too busy celebrating to recognize that we will no longer have someone sit down—every year, every semester, every week, every day—and develop a plan to provide us with the tools we need to become extraordinary.

We find ourselves finished with school, and then realize this special gift is gone. No one cares about what conversations we have tomorrow, whether they can lead us toward brilliant ideas or revelations, or what lessons we take home at the end of the quarter. There is no longer a syllabus outlining in clear detail everything we need to do to bring us closer to achieving our dreams. Nope, no longer do we have someone waking up each morning believing that his or her sole job is to make a difference in our lives.

In fact, after completing our formal education, we become responsible for our own continuing education. We are accountable to ourselves for ensuring we learn the necessary lessons that will help us be great in life. Now, following graduation, we are both the teacher and the student; it's our job to plot out what success looks like and define exactly how we will usher ourselves down a path to get there—quarter-by-quarter, month-by-month, week-by-week, and day-by-day. Nobody will do it for us.

Have you determined what you need to learn this year? Do you know your critical milestones or what you need to do to ensure that, without fail, you get to the next level?

You are the teacher. You are the gift. It's your responsibility to find the answers.

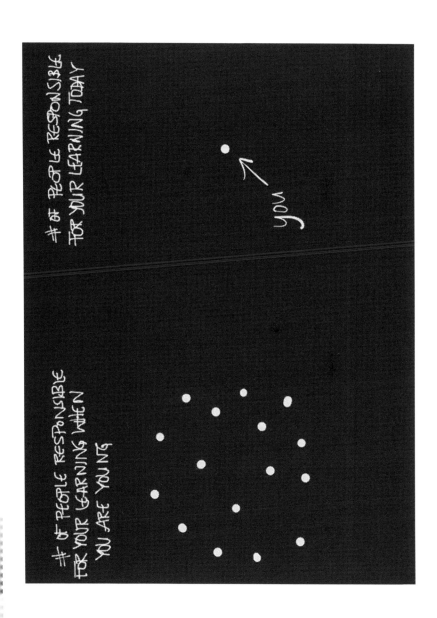

FIND YOUR SMALL MACHINE

*If you don't build your dream someone
will hire you to help build theirs.*
—*TONY GASKINS*

*Take time to mess around. Get lost. Wander.
You never know where it's going to lead you.*
—*AUSTIN KLEON*

Everyone with a big machine needs a small machine.

The big machine is your day job. It is the constant and stable pay-check. It's what you usually answer when people ask you what do you do.

The small machine, on the other hand, is made up of your solo projects. They are the entrepreneurial endeavors and personal passions you dabble with on the side, oftentimes when no one is looking.

The big machine and the small machine need each other; they share a symbiotic relationship. The big machine enables the small machine to happen. It funds the small machine and sometimes gives it credibility. This enables you to build a core skill set and knowledge base to help your small machine grow.

The small machine allows you to experiment, take risks, learn new things, and push boundaries. The small machine enables you to do things you could never do at your primary job. But at the end of the day, the small machine allows you to bring new perspective, insights, and ideas back to the big machine.

If you are not working full time to build your own dream, do not shackle yourself to your primary job. Get your small machines running so you can dream, test the waters, learn, and grow. If you do not have a small machine, find one. It will make you better at your big machine and, one day, it just may eliminate the need for the big machine to exist in the first place.

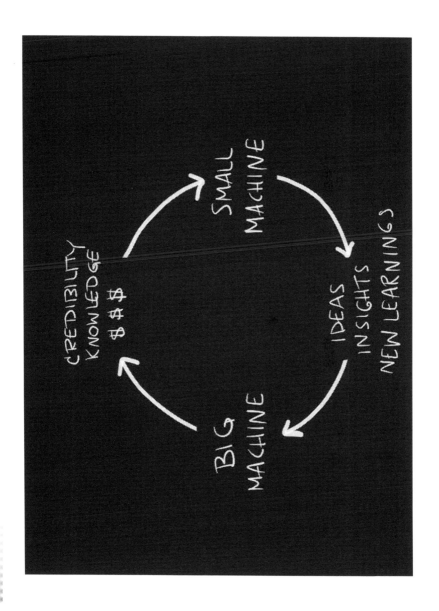

Burn Bridges

I walk slowly, but I never walk backward.
—Abraham Lincoln

Do not stumble over something behind you.
—Anonymous

Bridges are useful inventions. They help us get from point A to point B when the environment otherwise would bar our passage. We need bridges to close the gap between where we are and where we want to go. The danger of bridges is that they often give us the option of returning to home base.

Bridges offer us an easy way out. They allow us to change our minds and return to what feels safe. And when the going gets tough and we feel like quitting, bridges provide a welcome escape from the hard work of conquering new territory. Bridges allows us to question moving forward into the unknown because just a few steps back can return us to the familiar.

This may sound counterintuitive but, learn to burn your bridges. As you make progress toward your next destination, burn the pieces of bridge behind you that are no longer necessary or functional so you won't be tempted to use them again.

Without a bridge back to what feels safe, you will put up a bigger fight to reach your end destination. When there is not an option to run backward, you scrap harder to move forward. When your back is against the wall, you become determined to win by any means necessary.

Because of this reality, when my wife and I got married, we opted not to sign a prenuptial agreement. Although signing on the dotted line would have given us an added layer of comfort and protection for our unexpected future together, we did not want an insurance policy that would allow us to back out of our marriage. For us, failure was simply not an option; so we burned the bridge. Now, when "things hit the fan," we are forced to fight for our marriage because there is no easy bridge back to the single life.

Ancient military leaders also understood this truth and used it to their tactical advantage. They would often order their men to eliminate escape routes so troops would not be tempted to desert a battle before victory had been achieved. In times of war, leaders would commit their troops to an offensive by ordering them to burn their ships as soon as they reached enemy territory. The message to their troops was that there was no turning back. Winning was an imperative; conquer or die.

We can learn from these successful leaders by employing their winning strategy. If you really want to accomplish your dreams or bring your brilliant ideas to fruition, burn your bridges along the way so that you are left only with the option of battling until you emerge victorious.

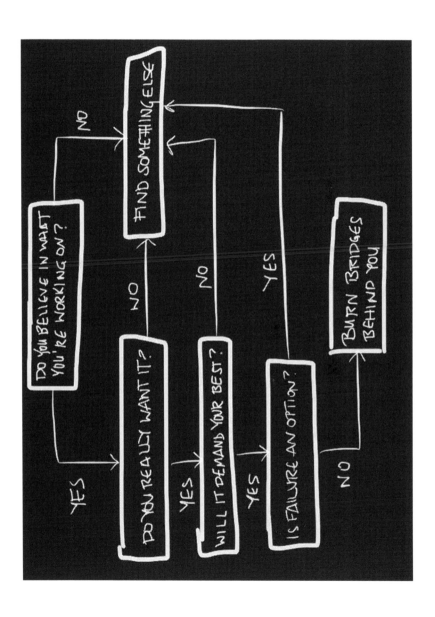

MAKE IT HAPPEN

Ideas and dreams without action are worthless. Power your ideas and dreams with your energy, not just your brain.

Schedule Someday

*If you dread tomorrow, it's because you don't know how to build
the present, and when you don't know how to build the present,
you tell yourself you can deal with it tomorrow, and it's a lost
cause anyway because tomorrow always ends up becoming today...*
—Muriel Barbery, *The Elegance of the Hedgehog*

*It's the oldest story in the world. One day you're seventeen
and planning for someday. And then quietly and without you ever
really noticing, someday is today. And that someday is yesterday.
And this is your life.*
—Nathan Scott, *One Tree Hill*

You should hate the word "someday." People rely on it too much.

"*Someday* I will get down to the weight I want."
"*Someday* I will start my own company."
"*Someday* I will travel around the world."
"Of course I will do it, *someday*."

Someday sounds good because it allows us to procrastinate. We use
this word to convince ourselves that we are serious about pursu-
ing our deepest goals and ambitions; yet, at the same time, we can
provide zero output to bring them to fruition. Someday allows us
to talk ourselves into believing that who we want to be is a priority,

when the truth is we would rather sit in the comfort of conformity than make an attempt to stretch ourselves. When we say someday, we trick ourselves into accepting that we are too busy today to do what our heart and mind are pleading for us to do.

Someday is really just a code word for never. Someday is where beautiful dreams and amazing ideas go to die.

If something matters, if it really, really matters to you, stop pushing it to someday. Stop assigning it to that fictitious eighth day of the weekly calendar that will never come, regardless of how often you mention its name.

Instead, pick a "freeze date."

A freeze date is the deadline for launching something. You can launch anytime prior to the freeze date, but you cannot push the freeze date back—it's frozen. Unmovable. When your freeze date comes around, that means it's time to get going. Not ready? Too bad! You knew the date was coming. And now that it is time to go, it is simply time to go.

Put a freeze date on the calendar for the day you will start chasing your dreams. Circle it. Tell your friends about it so they will encourage you and keep you motivated. And then, start preparing.

Get anything that might interfere with your timeline out the way. Go on vacation. Clear your mind. Watch every season of your favorite television show until you are all caught up. Do whatever you need so that when your freeze date shows up on your iPhone, you cannot come up with reasons for not starting. It is officially time to put yourself in the race. No excuses; you had time to prepare.

There are 365 days on a calendar. Do not wait for someday. Pick one.

DAYS OF THE WEEK

SUNDAY   THURSDAY

MONDAY   FRIDAY

TUESDAY   SATURDAY

WEDNESDAY   SOMEDAY

*PICK ANY ONE

EMBRACE SMALL BEGINNINGS

From small beginnings come great things.
—TRADITIONAL PROVERB

There are no big breaks. Only tiny drips of
effort that lead to waves of momentum.
—JEFF GOINS

Sometimes the best way to reach an extraordinary destination is to search for an extraordinarily small way to get started. Although this sounds counterintuitive, it is true. Our big, hairy, audacious goals do not always require us to take big, hairy, audacious actions in order to accomplish them. Sometimes, we just need to find the "small beginning."

A small beginning is the smallest action you can take that will in turn propel you toward your desired destination. There are two types of small beginnings: rippling and inching.

Rippling is all about building momentum. It is about performing the smallest action that will create a ripple effect that is difficult to stop. These actions are the pebbles we throw into the water that create a wave on the other side of the ocean.

Let's say you want to quit your job. Instead of worrying about disappointing your parents and wondering what your friends might say about your bright idea of leaving a good-paying position, boil the act of quitting down to the smallest possible action that could simultaneously create momentum for you. In this instance, the pebble toss could be as simple as sending a resignation email to your boss. Hitting Send on an email is something you've done millions of times before. The actual act will not be a difficult task for you—all it takes is one click of the mouse. Once you have sent it, you set the ripple affect in motion. HR knows. Office gossip begins. For all intents and purposes, you can start planning your good-bye speech because, for you, this job is over. Now you are off to the races.

Inching means taking small actions that aggregate and build toward a complete project over time. A famous film writer once told me that the secret to writing a great movie is simply to write every day. Apply this thinking to the various aspects of your life: small actions will eventually add up over time. An entrepreneur who dedicates his weekends to his company will have something to launch in a year. An individual who wants to go to graduate school and studies one hour every day will probably do well enough on the entrance exam to go to the program of his or her choice. The person who chooses to work out for at least thirty minutes every day will lose that gut he or she hates. It may not happen quickly, but inching ensures that it *will* happen.

Do not focus on the big goal—it will seem too overwhelming to tackle all at once and paralyze you. Find small steps you can take at the beginning that will give birth to a big, successful and rewarding future. Pick a dream or a project and start today. Boil things down to the tiniest action you can take that will catapult you to the next stage of your journey.

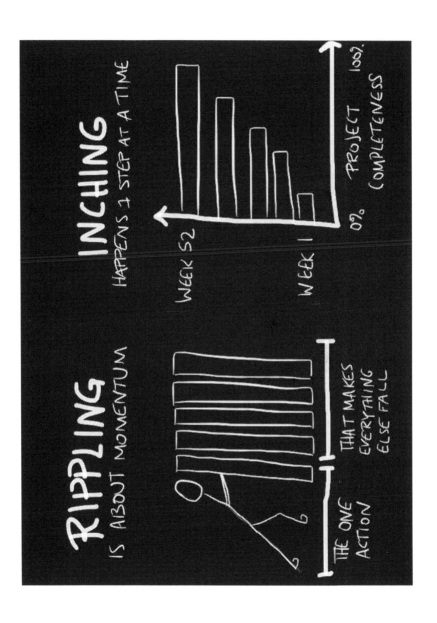

CREATE BAD CRAP

Nothing surpasses the beauty and elegance of a bad idea.
—CRAIG BRUCE

Ideas are like wandering sons.
They show up when you least expect them.
—BERN WILLIAMS

It's easy to admire genius. When we witness ingenuity, we praise those blessed with the gift for their abilities. But while it is easy to recognize and marvel at the extraordinary, we often miss—or are blind to—the reality of the work it took behind the scenes to get there.

True genius— in any medium— is always the result of a journey whose successes sit on the shoulders of various failed attempts. If genius is the end, making bad crap is the means. So, to excel at any craft, you have to be willing to make a lot of bad crap.

You need to get the bad crap out so that you can sort through it to find the nuggets of genius inside of you.

You need to get the bad crap out so that it can interact with the world and you can learn from the world's response to it.

You need to get the bad crap out because you are your toughest critic, and you may discover that the world does not actually think your idea is that bad at all.

A year ago I started "freewriting." Freewriting is a prewriting technique where you write down everything that comes to mind on a topic, without regard for grammar, style, or quality. The purpose of freewriting is to eliminate self-criticism before you get started—it squelches the desire to begin deleting and editing a sentence before you even know what the sentence wants itself to be—so that everything in your mind has the opportunity to compete for a place on your page. I've learned that, after a fifteen-minute freewriting exercise, I typically discover that my original idea was either half-baked or that there was another, better idea lurking around in my brain, waiting to be discovered. In order to get to the bigger idea, I have to allow myself to first rid my mind of all the junk that's cluttering up my thoughts.

Ultimately bad crap—once it is out the way—creates a space for brilliance to be born. If you want the world to see your genius, do not be afraid to get the bad crap out of your system.

Fight Daily

There's nothing like overcoming something that scares you so much. Nothing feels better.
—Laura Wilkinson

Don't be afraid of your fears. They're not there to scare you. They're there to let you know that something is worth it.
—C. JoyBell C.

Fear is a worthless emotion.

Initially, we humans developed fear to help us respond to the daily life-or-death threats that were common in our wild environment. Cavemen and hunters needed a mechanism to tell them to run or to protect themselves when a saber-toothed tiger or a lion was nearby. Fear enabled them to take action before it was too late.

But over the centuries, as humans moved from being hunter-gatherers on plains filled with woolly mammoths to office workers in cookie-cutter-house suburbs, the role fear once played in our lives became superfluous and even redundant. The dangers of the wild are no longer common in most of our daily routines and so fear is simply no longer necessary. Rather than accept extinction, however, fear has found a way to remain a part of our chemical makeup, causing us to have life-threatening responses to situations that are not really grave.

Sometimes we fail to fall in love despite being with a great person—not because being in love will kill us, but because we are afraid to have our feelings hurt. We stay in bad jobs—not because switching jobs will bring our demise, but because we are afraid to leave what is comfortable. We choose not to pursue our dreams—not because chasing our dreams is dangerous, but because we are simply afraid of failure.

Over time, fear has managed to evolve from being our survival aid to being our greatest archenemy.

Humans have always responded to fear in three distinct ways: by fighting, which means we "power up" and get ready for war; with flight, which means we strap on our Nikes and get the heck out of there as fast as we can; and by freezing, where our fear paralyzes us to the point that we literally cannot move. All too often we opt for the flight or freeze response. But, if you truly want the opportunity to pursue greatness, you will have to learn to respond to your daily fear mechanism with the desire to fight.

The good news is when you choose to fight, you have a partner. It's your own body. When you become afraid, the body alters itself, dialing up internal functions necessary to help you achieve success in a go-time situation. For example, your heartbeat increases. Your body also dials down other functions that do not have a role in leading you to victory. Your peripheral vision narrows and your hearing shuts down so you can focus. Use these to your benefit.

Get your heart rate up by encouraging and motivating yourself by working on something that excites you. Let your tunnel vision take over by prioritizing and concentrating on the steps that matter most for achieving your goal. And block out the useless noise around you—do not listen to anyone who will steer you off course. The rest is up to you. Roll up your sleeves. Strap on your gloves. And swing with everything you've got. Refuse to back down until you have emerged victorious from whatever battle you are fighting. You have little to lose and a whole lot to gain.

Letting fear stop you is bowing to an out-of-date adversary. Fear's only reason for being with you today should be to help you fight harder than you have ever fought before. If you let fear stop you, you are the only one that loses.

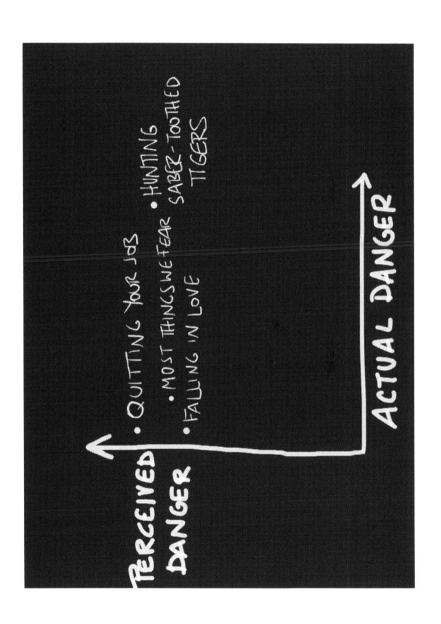

GET TO CAN

It always seems impossible until it's done.
—*NELSON MANDELA*

Never think there is anything impossible for the soul. It is the greatest heresy to think so. If there is sin, this is the only sin; to say that you are weak, or others are weak.
—*SWAMI VIVEKANANDA*

There will always be an excuse for why you *cannot* do something. There is the timeline problem. Or the money issue. Or the supervisor who always manages to get in the way. Whether it's your dream job, a project, or a big idea, "I can't" always finds a way into the equation.

Although you will always be able to find a reason you *can't*, in order to get the most out of this life, you will have to learn to find reasons you *can*.

Getting to *can* is not always a simple task. It might require late nights, more resources, or creative solutions that have yet to be developed. But getting to *can* is always an option.

At work, I never let a conversation end with "I can't." Whenever we get stuck on a difficult problem, I ask the team to tell me—no matter how crazy the answer—what it would take to overcome it. Tell me you need me to hire ten people to work through the night. Tell me that, in order to meet the deadline, we can only finish the most important 90 percent of the original task. Heck, tell me you need a purple unicorn to get the job done. I do not care what the answer is—just tell me what it will take to get to *can*. Once you know realistically what it will take to achieve your goal, then you can decide whether the tradeoffs to get to *can* are worth it or not.

Too often, we settle for *can't*—when *can* is always possible.

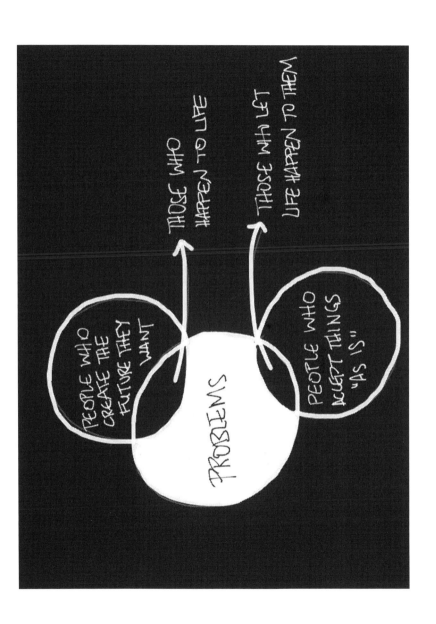

FOCUS ON YOUR WATER

Hard is not about sweat or time, hard is about finishing the rare, valuable, risky task that few complete.
—SETH GODIN

Chuck your to-do list, make a not-to-do list.
—ANONYMOUS

Every step in a project is not equal; some steps are "cupcakes" and some steps are "water."

Cupcakes are the steps that are not essential to getting the project done. They may be fun. And they may make you feel like you have accomplished something. But at the end of the day, they do not really bring your dream to reality.

Today, our lives are crammed with cupcakes. Twitter updates are cupcakes. Facebook updates are cupcakes. You can tweet and share every day for the next year, but unless your project hinges on a stellar Twitter feed or Facebook page, neither will get you any closer to seeing your vision manifested.

Water refers to the steps in a project that are the difference makers. These are the three to five most important steps that, if you do not get them done, will kill the entire project.

Everything depends on water: it is the life source. If you are starting a new product line, water is getting the product right. If you are writing a book, water is generating quality content. If you are launching a new service, water is making those dreaded sales calls so you can get your first customers.

Water steps are the steps the project cannot live without. They demand your best energy because they are also usually the hardest to complete. They are the efforts that take you out of your comfort zone. They are often the milestones that put you in the pathway of rejection. They are the most difficult steps to force yourself to do; but, in the end, they are the *only* steps that matter.

Before you give your energy to something you are working on today, ask yourself: Is this a cupcake or is it water? Everybody likes cupcakes, but water will determine if your project lives or dies.

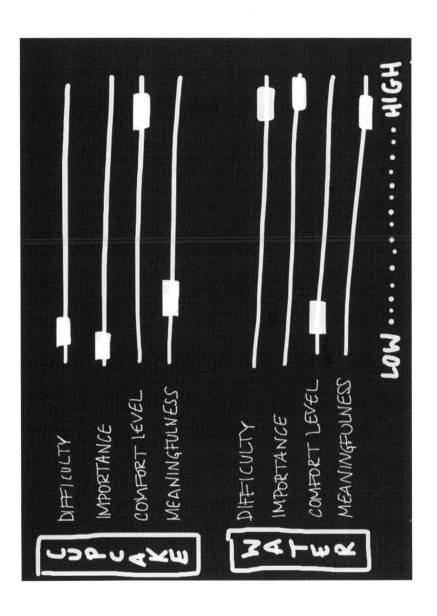

Aim for Done

The surest hindrance of success is to have too high a standard of refinement in our own minds, or too high an opinion of the judgment of the public. He who is determined not to be satisfied with anything short of perfection will never do anything to please himself or others.

—William Hazlitt

If you wait too long for the perfect moment, the perfect moment will pass you by.

—Anonymous

All too often our inner genius generates brilliant ideas our inner critic never lets us birth. Our desire to be perfect before we expose ourselves to the world prevents us from allowing our best ideas to ever see the light of day. The best of what we have to offer the world is indefinitely put on hold when we tell ourselves things like:

I am going to start my blog this year—I'm just waiting to perfect my voice first.

I am going to launch my company—just as soon as the timing is right.

I will start selling my world-famous cake—just as soon as I perfect the recipe.

Nothing is ever perfect. Nothing is ever finished. We now live in a world of perpetual beta, where things are always ever-evolving. There will always be room for growth and improvement; perfection will never come. Claiming you're in pursuit of perfection is just another excuse to never show your real self to the world.

Ideas that exist merely as thoughts and never become things will only grow up to be a fraction of what they are supposed to be. It is not until your idea interacts with the universe and is punched, kicked, hugged and kissed by the world that it can ultimately figure out and evolve into its true form. Yes, there may be a bit of risk and failure involved; however, risk and failure are the twins needed to bring improvement, understanding and advancement to any situation in life.

If you are serious about getting something off the ground, do not aim for perfection. Make it the best you can with the information and resources you have available now and aim for "done" instead. It will not be flawless. It will not be pristine. But who cares? Push Go. Hit Send. Launch your creation or product into the universe. Once your idea is out there, listen, learn and evolve your idea into what it is telling you it wants to be.

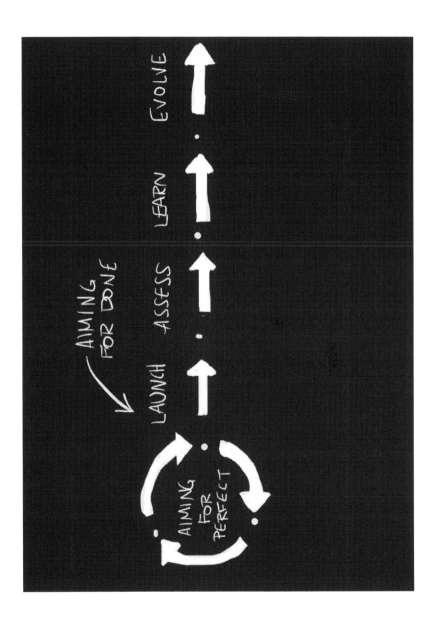

PARTING WORDS

Squeeze The Heck Out Of The Middle

Thank you for taking the time to read this book. I sincerely hope you got more out of it than you anticipated. As we close our time together, I want to leave you with these parting words that, for me, summarize the essence of this book:

Everything has a beginning and an end. Life is no different. Your personal beginning (birth) and end (death) are determined for you; they are fixed and out of your control. What is in your control is what you choose to do with the unchangeable time in between: the middle.

The middle is where you get to enjoy life's possibilities. The middle is where you generate lasting impact. The middle is, essentially, where you and all the magic happen.

Do not miss out on the middle. Unleash your personal magic. Don't be afraid to challenge conventional wisdom. And make something truly amazing happen along the way.

Do not let life pass you by: Squeeze the heck out of the middle.

EXIST NO MORE MANIFESTO

SOME PEOPLE THEY ACCEPT THE WORLD THAT HAS BEEN HANDED TO THEM AND CALL IT FINAL.
SETTLE;
THEY PLAY A PASSIVE ROLE IN THIS GAME CALLED LIFE.
I AM NOT ONE OF THOSE PEOPLE.

I BELIEVE IMPOSSIBLE IS NOTHING; THAT HAPPINESS IS A GIFT GIVEN BY THE CHOICES I MAKE; THAT THE CONVENTIONS STANDING BETWEEN ME AND MY DREAMS ARE SIMPLY RULES MEANT TO BE BROKEN. I AM NOT AFRAID OF THE UNCHARTERED PATH; AUTOPILOT IS NEVER MY PREFERRED MEANS OF TRAVEL.

I AM PART OF THE **DREAM MAKERS,** THE **PASSION CHASERS,** THE **IDEA CREATORS.** I AM THE ARCHITECT OF THE FUTURE I IMAGINE, THE AUTHOR OF THE STORY I WANT TO LIVE.

YOU ONLY GET ONE CHANCE TO LEAVE A DENT IN THIS WORLD. **MY CHANCE** LUCKY FOR ME, **IS NOW.** I'VE GOT ONE SHOT TO LIVE AND I'VE MADE MY CHOICE. **I WILL EXIST NO MORE.**

WWW.EXISTNOMORE.COM

103

What To Do Next

1. Visit existnomore.com to find more inspiration.

2. Cut your favorite pictures out of the book and pin them up as reminders.

3. Close your eyes and answer this question: What is your art? Once you know the answer, go do it.

4. Have a "Sweet Spot Party" where everyone creates a list of his or her talents and passions. Then brainstorm with each other all of the jobs you can imagine where each person can put his or her respective talents and passions to work. Get creative.

5. Buy the book, StrengthsFinder 2.0.

6. Spend two weeks working on that idea you have been sitting on. Do not pause to ask anyone what he or she thinks of the idea (including yourself) until the two weeks are over.

7. Make a "not-to-do" list.

8. Identify a dream, goal or project you have set to the side for a long time. Find the "small beginning" that will help you get started.

9. Define the 1-3 things you want to learn over the next 9 weeks. Then go learn them.

10. Take a week off of work and get your small machine up and running. Launch it to the world and see what happens.

BOOKS WORTH READING

- StrengthsFinder 2.0 by Tom Rath

- The Alchemist by Paulo Coelho

- Rework by Jason Fried and David Heinemeier Hansson

- Steal Like an Artist: 10 Things Nobody Told You About Being Creative by Austin Kleon

- Do The Work!: Overcome Resistance and Get Out of Your Own Way by Steven Pressfield

- The Flinch by Julien Smith

- Ignore Everybody by Hugh MacLeod

- Tribes: We Need You To Lead Us by Seth Godin

ACKNOWLEDGEMENTS

To God, the Father—Without you, none of this would be possible. I am humbled by your presence in my life. I will continue to follow wherever You lead me.

To Tanya—Thanks for never being upset during all of those late nights and early mornings when you woke up to an empty bed because I was hiding in some back room trying to get this book out. Thanks for being my eyes every day and having the courage to tell me when my doodles and writings were crap.

To Dad—Thanks for spending so much time with the book and ensuring that I put my best foot forward. When I was "aiming for done," you helped me see that spending a little more time would take it one step closer to perfect. Thanks for pushing me. I'm glad we can add this book to the list of great things we've done together in our lifetimes.

To Victor—Thanks for the free creativity and inspiration sessions. Thanks for always being willing to lend an ear and a brain to make any of the projects I work on great. You are one-of-a-kind. The book cover and front graphic are dope—thanks for hooking them up.

To my blog readers—Thanks for reading the blog over the course of the last few years and being patient with me as I perfected my voice. Your emails, your Facebook messages, your "thank yous" have singlehandedly kept me going over the last few years.

To the originators of every idea in this book—No idea is truly original; I borrowed from so many of you. I did my best to give credit where possible and tried to show my readers that I am not the first person to play around with the topics in this book. Thank you for your inspiration. Through this work and others, I hope your legacy continues to live on.

To the creators of the tools I used to write this book. I'm not sure how I would have gotten this book done without you. Evernote you're amazing; I used your app to organize EVERYTHING (literally everything). And fiftythree, your Paper drawing app has opened my eyes to a whole new level of creativity; thank you for inspiring me to draw again.

To anyone I may have forgotten to thank…Thank you. I love you.

ABOUT THE AUTHOR

Detavio Samuels is a servant leader dedicated to helping people and brands unleash their magic. At the young age of 32 he operates as the President of GlobalHue-Detroit, the nation's premier total market advertising agency, where he manages relationships with the agency's blue chip clientele. Outside of GlobalHue, Detavio travels across the nation speaking to people of all ages and encouraging them to live up to the awesomeness that is inside of them.

Detavio is a graduate of Stanford University, where he received his master's degrees in Business Administration and Education. Detavio is also a graduate of Duke University where he completed his undergraduate work and became a proud member of Kappa Alpha Psi.

Currently, Detavio lives in New York City with his beautiful wife, Tanya. Together they are focused on loving each other and living a life that reflects the presence of God in their lives.

You can follow his blog or contact Detavio Samuels at detavio.com

Made in the USA
Charleston, SC
23 October 2014